Islay: ships, smoke and spirit barley, boats and barrels
Guthrie Hutton

C000178460

Peat, seen here being gathered in the 1950s, was once an essential fuel for the islanders,
but with distilling's rise to prominence it has acquired almost mythical status for its role in flavouring whisky.

Most Islay distilleries have their names painted in very large black letters on the face of very white buildings as this 1930s photograph of visitors to Ardbeg shows.

© Guthrie Hutton, 2013
First published in the United Kingdom, 2013,
by Stenlake Publishing Ltd.
54-58 Mill Square, Catrine, KA5 6RD
01290 551122
www.stenlake.co.uk

Printed by
Blissetts, Unit 1, Shield Drive,
West Cross Industrial Park, Brentford, TW8 9EX

ISBN 9781840336375

The publishers regret that they cannot supply copies of any pictures featured in this book.

Acknowledgements

Without the help of Jim and Linda Brown, this little book would have been much diminished and more difficult to compile. I must therefore thank them for their considerable contribution. I must also thank the people of Islay, always friendly – that little wave for every passing motorist is wonderful – and ever ready to answer my seemingly obscure questions and thus add a little to every story. Numerous web sites also proved to be a great source of building up stories, as did the resources of the Mitchell Library in Glasgow. And another thing made the research a real pleasure – well you have to sample the whisky to know what to write about!

Further Reading

The books listed below were used by the author during his research. With the exception of *Old Islay* none are available from Stenlake Publishing; please contact your local bookshop or reference library.

Banks, Iain, *Raw Spirit*, 2004.
Barnard, Alfred, The Whisky Distilleries of the United Kingdom, 1887 (reprint 2008).
Carmichael, Gilbert, *Old Islay*, 1998.
Duckworth, C. and Langmuir, D., *West Highland Steamers*, 1967.
Lo Bao, Phil and Hutchison, Peter, *BEAline to the Islands*, 2002.
McCrorie, Ian, *Royal Road to the Isles*, 2001.
Moir, Peter and Crawford Ian, *Argyll Shipwrecks*, 1994.
Museum of Islay Life, *The Isle of Islay*, 1998.

Newton, Norman S., *Islay*, 1988.
Pennant, Thomas, *A Tour in Scotland 1772*, pub. 1774.
Ritchie, Graham and Harman, Mary, *Exploring Scotland's Heritage: Argyll and the Western Isles*, 1985.
Smith, Gavin D., *The Secret Still*, 2002.
Society of Antiquaries of Scotland, *Telling Scotland's Story*, 2013.
Storrie, Margaret C., *Islay: Biography of an Island*, 1981.
Walker, Frank Arneil, *The Buildings of Scotland: Argyll and Bute*, 2000.

Introduction

Islay is rich in many things, like scenery, wildlife and archaeological mysteries. It also has a history of warrior clans, a turbulent time when the MacDonald chiefs styled themselves as Lords of the Isles and ruled over Scotland's western seaboard with fire and sword. Islay was the centre of their universe, a kingdom within a kingdom, but eventually the Stuart monarchs in Edinburgh lost patience and clipped Clan Donald's wings. Islay slipped into obscurity, while Clan Campbell moved in to complete the MacDonald's discomfort. With their hold on the island consolidated, a new Campbell family took over as lairds and began a series of agricultural reforms that transformed the island's social structure and land use. During this time an industry with its roots firmly planted in illegality became established: distilling.

Distilling is essentially simple. Barley is steeped in water and spread on a floor. Germination starts and is then stopped by heating the grain over a peat fire. It is now malt, which is ground and mixed with water at a controlled temperature, completing the process of converting the starch to sugar. The sugar dissolves in the liquid, which is run off into large vats. Yeast is added and fermentation takes place, converting the sugar into alcohol. Heated in a large still, the liquid is vaporised, then condensed and the resultant spirit is left to mature for three or more years in carefully selected wooden casks. It is the same process worldwide, but something

glorious and mysterious makes Islay whisky different. It could be the water, the peat, the sea air, the barrels, local expertise, or a combination of any of these factors, but whatever it is Islay whisky is special and because of that, the island name is held in awe and wonder the world over.

Making all that whisky would have been faintly pointless if it could not be got off the island and sold and the same was true of the products of other industries like farming, fishing and weaving. Initially small sailing craft, known on the west coast as gabbarts, scuttled back and forth, but with the advent of steam they were superseded by puffers. Drovers used another method, driving their animals through Jura, with ferries linking the islands and the mainland. Steamer operators eschewed this route, preferring longer sailings. As roads and vehicles developed, boats and piers were adapted, so that when cargo ships met their nemesis, it came in the form of ferries and articulated lorries.

With ships being adapted to changing needs and aircraft added to the transport mix, tourism has grown. People come to enjoy the scenery, the wildlife, the history, or to play golf and bag distilleries. It is a rare mix of old and new that makes Islay itself like a good whisky; a place to savour, to gladden the eye and awake the senses.

Lagavulin (the name can be roughly translated as mill by the little hollow) is the middle one of the three south coast distilleries. It is seen here from the north in an early twentieth century picture.

For a long time much of the whisky made on Islay was used for blending. Only recently, with the growth in popularity of single malts, have individual distilleries become well known. The exception to this was Laphroaig, which for a long time was marketed on its own, although it did contribute to one notable blend, Islay Mist. It is the most westerly of three distilleries along a two-mile stretch of the island's south coast. They are all famed for strong peaty malt whisky, but the one that traditionally has excited the strongest opinions is Laphroaig, attracting descriptions that vary from likening it to something medicinal to unalloyed praise (your scribe is in the latter category). If opinions of Laphroaig vary so too do accounts of when the distillery was built, which might indicate origins that may not have been entirely legal. Set up by brothers Donald and Alexander Johnston it was in existence by 1826 and remained under family control until the 1960s when it was acquired by Long John International and subsequently became part of Fortune Brands' spirits arm Beam Global.

4

As well as being the site of a great distillery, Lagavulin Bay is also the location of Dunivaig Castle, seen here as a gaunt ruin in a picture from the early 1900s. The castle was a stronghold of the Macdonalds of Islay during their time as Lords of the Isles. Stripped of the title in 1493 by King James IV, their influence waned through the following century and the castle became the focus of much plotting and scheming until 1614/15 when Sir John Campbell ousted the Macdonalds from the island. It's not hard to imagine the castle's occupants during those turbulent times enjoying the occasional dram and it seems likely that whisky has been made around Lagavulin for centuries. In his splendid essays exploring *The Whisky Distilleries of the United Kingdom* the journalist Alfred Barnard dispelled any doubt that illegal distilling and smuggling were a way of life here when he suggested that it was going strong in 1742, with ten bothies engaged in making what he described as 'moonlight' – as distinct to 'daylight' or duty paid whisky.

The ten moonlight-making bothies recorded at Lagavulin by Alfred Barnard were superseded in 1816 and 1817 by two legal establishments, one of which was set up by John Johnston and the other by Archibald Campbell. The two were later amalgamated and in the 1880s, when Barnard paid his visit, the owner was James Logan Mackie & Co. Perhaps the most prominent member of the family was Peter Mackie, also known as 'restless Pete' who created the famous White Horse Whisky – a blend of 40 grain and malt whiskies with Lagavulin at its heart. Peter (later Sir Peter) Mackie also set up a traditional distillery at Lagavulin known as the Malt Mill and equipped it with distinctive pear-shaped stills, which have remained a feature of Lagavulin despite the closure of the Malt Mill in 1960. Following Sir Peter's death in 1924 the distillery was taken over by Distillers Company Limited and subsequently became part of the drinks group Diageo.

Like its neighbour at Lagavulin, Ardbeg was, in Alfred Barnard's words, 'a noted haunt of smugglers'. Romantic to some, villains to others, these characters foiled the attentions of the authorities for years, but after a long cat-and-mouse operation the excise men were finally able to move in while the gang was away selling their whisky to raid the stills, seize the illicit spirit and destroy the operation. This activity can only have enhanced the whisky-making reputation of the locality and in 1815 a member of the local McDougal family established the Ardbeg Distillery. The family retained an interest in the distillery until 1977 when it was sold to Hiram Walker. In 1981 disaster struck for the lovers of Ardbeg: the distillery was mothballed. It remained closed during two further changes of ownership, but in 1997 distilling was started up again. Enthusiasts responded by forming a fan club, or committee, to ensure a more certain future for their favourite dram.

Ardbeg, Lagavulin and Laphroaig distilleries were all situated on the Kildalton Estate, the property of John Ramsay. He acquired the land and all that went with it in 1855 and later extended his holdings by adding the Oa Estate. His grand mansion, Kildalton House, sometimes also known as Kildalton Castle, was built in the late 1860s to the designs of architect John Burnett. Situated just over a mile to the east of Ardbeg it comprised (on the ground floor) an outer and inner hall, dining room, drawing room, library, smoking, billiard and gun rooms as well as the kitchen, scullery and servants' quarters. The bedrooms, bathrooms and toilet facilities were upstairs. There was a separate wing containing the nurseries and some bedrooms. Two more bedrooms were located in the tower and anyone gaining access to the tower roof could enjoy superb views. Service facilities attached to the house included a dairy, laundry, extensive stabling and a coach house.

If the living was easy at Kildalton House, communicating with the outside world from this island idyll could scarcely have been simpler as this little cottage situated at the lodge gates housed a post and telegraph office. The contents of any letters that passed through it can only be guessed at: the weather, the scenery, the midges, but a few miles to the east was one special feature that must surely have inspired a few words, the Kildalton Cross. Standing beside the ruins of the Old Parish Church, it is one of Scotland's finest early Christian crosses and is perhaps the most impressive historical artefact on Islay. Carved from a single slab of stone it dates from the second half of the eighth century when Islay was part of the Dalriadic kingdom that also included the Island of Iona where crosses of a similar style and date also survive.

Port Ellen, the principal settlement site in the south of the island, was begun in 1821 by the laird of Islay, Walter Frederick Campbell. He named it after his first wife, Eleanor, later shortened to Ellen. His own middle name graces the buildings facing the bay, Frederick Crescent. It is seen here looking east in a view taken from the junction with Charlotte Street. The large building on the right was formerly the police station. In the distance, in the middle of the picture, is the United Free Church, built in 1911 to replace the old Free Church. It had occupied a site to the north of the village since 1845, but was superseded following the amalgamation of the United Presbyterian and Free Churches in 1900. The United Free Church building itself became surplus to requirements after the reconciliation of the Presbyterian churches in 1929 and St John's Church of Scotland, further round the bay, became the principal place of worship.

Walter Campbell chose his spot well, beside the sheltered bay formed by Loch Leodamais and the larger bay to the west where the beach, Traigh Gheighsgeir, on the right of this picture formed the shore. Charlotte Street, the road in the foreground, was named after Walter Campbell's mother and is also the main road linking Port Ellen with the north of the island. Facing the beach, on the left, is the White Hart Hotel, one of two large hotels in the village. The other, the Islay Hotel, can be seen in the distance, just to the right of centre, standing tall above the other buildings. Just out of the picture on the left, is the imposing Ramsay Hall erected in 1902 by Iain Ramsay as a memorial to his father John Ramsay, the laird of Kildalton Estate, who died in 1892 and, according to the inscription above the door, 'lived in and loved Islay'. Had the picture also been extended to the right, it would have included the pier.

Port Ellen Pier is seen here in September 1949, with the puffer *Pibroch* alongside. These splendid little ships, made famous in the stories of Para Handy and the *Vital Spark*, brought coal, empty barrels and other essentials to Islay's piers and took out barrels of whisky, but *Pibroch* was different because she was the only puffer actually owned by a distillery, the identity of which was evident to anyone who noticed the little white horse mounted on her masthead. Built in 1923 at Scott's yard at Bowling on the Clyde, she worked between Glasgow and Islay, through the Crinan Canal, until 1957 when she was replaced. The new boat, a diesel coaster also named *Pibroch* and sporting a white horse emblem at the masthead, remained in service until 1989. The old puffer was sold to new owners and renamed *Texa*, after the little island off the south coast of Islay. Her name was changed again, to *Cumbrae Lass*, before she was broken up in 1967.

Lochiel, the ship seen here at Port Ellen Pier, was the fourth boat in the David MacBrayne fleet to bear the name. Built at William Denny's shipyard at Dumbarton and launched in April 1939, she was intended for the Islay service, but initially worked between Oban and Fort William until the pier at West Loch Tarbert was modified to suit her. The route between the loch and the island was first used in 1878 when the *Glencoe* worked it for a few months before being replaced for the following season by the first MacBrayne steamer to be named *Lochiel*. She in turn was superseded by a succession of other vessels until *Glencoe* returned to the route in 1892. The now venerable steamer (she had been built as the *Mary Jane* in 1846) continued to ply between the island and mainland until 1905 when a purpose-built steamer, *Pioneer*, took over. In the background of the picture, behind the bow section of the ship, is Port Ellen Distillery.

Port Ellen Distillery was established in 1825 in the wake of the 1823 Excise Act, a key legislative component in the development of the modern whisky industry. The Act required distillers to pay an annual license fee, but crucially specified a minimum size for a still at 40 gallons and reduced the duty paid on a gallon of spirits. At a stroke the incentives for smuggling and illicit distillation were removed and the path set for large-scale operations to become established, many on the sites of former illegal stills. Some time before the early twentieth century, when this picture was taken, the distillery was owned and operated by the estate proprietor and the whisky known as Ramsay, Islay. Distilling ceased at Port Ellen in 1929, restarted after reconstruction in 1967, but stopped again in 1983. A large maltings that went into production in 1974 continued in operation after the closure of the distillery supplying malt to most of Islay's distilleries, but tailored to their different requirements.

Cairnmore, just beyond Port Ellen Distillery on the road to the Oa, was a dower house of the Kildalton Estate. For a dwelling that was not the principal residence of the estate it was quite a place. The ground floor consisted of a dining room and library and the usual domestic offices of servant's hall, butler's pantry, kitchen and scullery. The drawing room, principal bedrooms, bathroom and toilet were on the first floor along with the housemaid's pantry. The upper floor consisted of eight guest bedrooms, three servants' bedrooms and a heated linen cupboard. There was stabling for six horses, a harness room, two heated coach houses, a coachman's house and accommodation for three other men. The property was even equipped with an acetylene gas plant, which provided hot water for the heating system, and the water was drawn from the same source that supplied Port Ellen Distillery.

Spelled with two letters, only the first of which is pronounced, the Oa is a peninsula that, when looked at on a map, is almost square. With Ireland to the south and America to the west, it juts out into a turbulent sea with a rugged shoreline that has claimed many ships like the *Harald*. An iron-hulled sailing ship, she was on passage between Wales and Norway in August 1909 when she ran into a fog and onto the rocks. On land, the Oa became part of the estates acquired in the mid-nineteenth century by John Ramsay who encouraged his impoverished tenants to emigrate. His methods were benign compared to the actions of 'clearance' landlords elsewhere, and he followed his former tenants to Canada to see how they were faring, but it did mean that the population of the Oa was significantly reduced. Some of the places that the people left behind had names ending in 'bus' - Cregabus, Risabus, Kinnabus - a suffix with Norse origins that is common throughout Islay and means farmstead.

By 1917, when the United States of America came into the First World War, the original combatants had become familiar with the conflict's capacity to generate high casualty figures. Americans were not so inured and so, when two ships carrying their servicemen were sunk, one on 5th February 1918 and the other on 6th October that year, it was a huge shock. The ships were both peacetime passenger liners pressed into Admiralty service. The first, HMS *Tuscania*, was torpedoed seven miles off the Mull of Oa and sank with some 200 American casualties while the other, HMS *Otranto*, collided with another ship in a fog and went down off Islay with the loss of 351 Americans. Over 130 British seamen also perished, but these tragedies had a bigger impact in America and to provide a fitting memorial the American National Red Cross erected a monument on the Oa in 1920. The people in the picture must have gone to see it soon after its completion.

Machrie Golf Course occupies an area of undulating sandy hillocks on the shores of Laggan Bay, or the Big Strand, about four miles north of Port Ellen. It was designed by Willie Campbell of Bridge of Weir and opened to wide acclaim in May 1891. In laying out the holes, Willie Campbell took full advantage of the terrain to produce a course of championship quality. Numerous natural sand traps, burns, gullies, sunken roads and broken ground made the going tough for the unwary, but the hole that struck awe into early commentators was the third, known as Mount Zion. Three perfectly executed shots, with the unsophisticated clubs and balls of the day, were needed to reach the green, which was protected in front by a burn in a gully. The green itself sat on an island-like plateau with ground falling away on all sides and if a golfer overshot they found themselves on the beach. The splendid views of the bay were probably scant compensation. The match shown in the picture has reached a hole known as the Scotsman's Maiden, which was similar to the famous Maiden Hole at the Royal St. George's Course at Sandwich in Kent.

Machrie Hotel, Port-Ellen, Isle of Islay.

D. C. MACINTYRE, *Proprietor.*   *Telegrams: " Machrie, Port-Ellen."*

After testing their prowess at both golf and arithmetic, weary players could savour a post-game dram in the nineteenth hole, conveniently situated in the adjacent Machrie Hotel, a former farmhouse. Described in a 1930s brochure, when Mr D. Campbell McIntyre was the proprietor, it had a quaint, old world exterior that belied a very up-to-date interior. Each of the public rooms had modern, tasteful furnishings. There was a ladies' drawing room, a large lounge and smoke room, and a dining room where meals made with fresh produce from the home farm were varied, well cooked and well served. Private sitting rooms were available and every bedroom was the last word in comfort. Guests who did not want to play golf could go fishing on the island's many lochs, or shoot some moorland birds. There was less risk to the wildlife from those residents who preferred to go for a walk on the seven-mile long beach.

With the aim of delivering newspapers to remote places on the morning of publication, Midland and Scottish Air Ferries Ltd. started the first scheduled air service in Scotland, between Renfrew and Campbeltown on 18th April 1933. The first passengers were carried on 27th April and the service was extended to Islay on 16th May and to Belfast two weeks later. The first landing strip on the island was the beach opposite Bridgend, but by the time this advertisement appeared in May 1934, the 'aerodrome' had been relocated to a grass strip at Duich. A couple of days before the passenger service began a fisherman, John McDermid, was found to be in danger of contracting peritonitis from a perforated stomach, so his doctor sent an urgent telegram requesting the assistance of an aircraft. Midland and Scottish Air Ferries answered the call, collecting the patient from the beach at Bridgend and taking him to Glasgow in what is regarded as the first use of an air ambulance in Scotland.

John Sword, the owner of Midland and Scottish Air Ferries, was also general manager of Western Scottish Motor Traction, a conflict of interest that caused him to pull out of running air services, with the one to Islay ceasing at the end of September 1934. Two months later Northern and Scottish Airways started the service up again, initially flying in to Duich, but in 1935 moved to a new airfield further south at Glenegedale, which is seen here shortly after its inauguration; the steps to help passengers get on and off the aircraft can be seen in the left foreground. The other pictures also show the airfield and some early aircraft to land on Islay. Initially the landing strip at Glenegedale was grass covered, but during the Second World War a tarmac runway was laid for the Royal Air Force and passenger aircraft have been using it ever since. Northern and Scottish Airways became Scottish Airways in 1937, but when the Civil Aviation Act of 1946 came into force it became part of the newly nationalized British European Airways.

Mulindry, in the centre of the island, is, like Lagavulin, a place with milling origins in its name. It is seen here in a view looking south across Mulindry Bridge, with the little school on the left and the hill known as Cnoc Cro a Mhail behind. Tree growth since the picture was taken would make it a difficult view to replicate. The bridge spans Islay's principal river, the Laggan, which was tapped near here in the 1820s to supply one of Islay's least successful distilleries. It failed because the owner apparently enjoyed his product too much. Overlooking Mulindry is one of Islay's most impressive archaeological sites, Dun Nosebridge. A grass-grown hill fort measuring approximately 95 feet by 55 feet, it crowns the ridge overlooking the Laggan Valley, with the steeply sloping hillside as defence on one side and a system of banks and ditches protecting the other three sides. The site is thought to date from the first millennium AD, but without excavation this is not definitive.

Over the years, little schools like that at Mulindry were closed and education provision was concentrated at the main population centres, like Bowmore, where Bowmore School was built a few years after the passing of the Education Act in 1872. Primary and secondary schools have since grown to occupy a prominent site, with further extensions built in the 1980s having roof ventilators made to look like the pagoda-shaped vents of a distillery. Taken in 1952, from a spot in front of where those later extensions were built, this view looks down School Street towards the village and harbour. The distillery is on the left although the only obvious element of it is the factory chimney on the edge of the picture. A large silo and other structures have since made the street's proximity to the distillery more apparent.

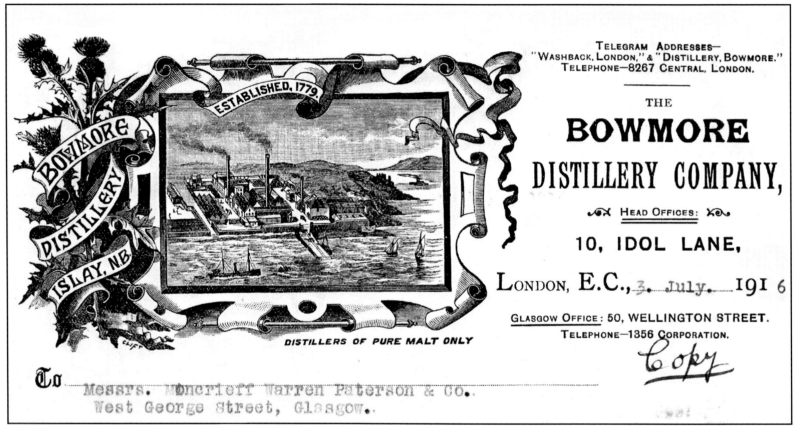

TELEGRAM ADDRESSES—
"WASHBACK, LONDON," & "DISTILLERY, BOWMORE."
TELEPHONE—8267 CENTRAL, LONDON.

THE

BOWMORE

DISTILLERY COMPANY,

HEAD OFFICES:

10, IDOL LANE,

LONDON, E.C., 3. July. 1916

GLASGOW OFFICE: 50, WELLINGTON STREET.

TELEPHONE—1356 CORPORATION.

Copy

ESTABLISHED, 1779.

BOWMORE DISTILLERY ISLAY, NB

DISTILLERS OF PURE MALT ONLY

To

Messrs. Moncrieff Warren Paterson & Co.
West George Street, Glasgow.

Bowmore Distillery is one of the oldest in Scotland, established by the Simson family in 1779. It was bought about 1837 by members of the Mutter family and they carried out some significant improvements. For a brief period they also owned a small cargo vessel, the *James Mutter*, which was sold to David MacBrayne in 1889 and renamed *Texa*, evidently the default name given to steamers formerly owned by distillers (see page 12). The distillery was still in the Mutter's ownership in the 1880s when Alfred Barnard paid it a visit. In his report he didn't hide his admiration, praising the mix of innovative and traditional practices, some of which, like the double-headed still, were unique. He was also impressed by the size of the operation and in particular the lade bringing water from the River Laggan, five miles away as the crow flies, but significantly longer to cope with the lie of the land.

Following the Mutter family, J. B. Sheriff of Campbeltown owned the distillery for a few years before selling out to a consortium led by Joseph Robert Holmes. They ran the operation until 1925 when J. B. Sheriff moved back in and coupled their own name with the whisky as Sheriff Bowmore. Distilling was stopped during the Second World War and some of the buildings were used by the Royal Air Force as an operations centre for flying boats that were based on Loch Indaal and used for convoy protection. Restarted after the war, the distillery was bought in 1963 by Stanley P. Morrison who renamed the whisky, Morrison's Bowmore. The Morrison name continued to be associated with the business after 1994 when it was taken over by Japanese drinks company Suntory. The distillery's ability to treasure the old while embracing the new has been demonstrated in more recent times with a swimming pool, part of the Mactaggart Leisure Centre, being set up in an old bonded warehouse and provided with waste heat.

In common with the other principal towns and villages of Islay, Bowmore was established by the landowner in an attempt to effect a range of improvements. The distinction for Bowmore is that it was the first such development, put in hand by Daniel Campbell in 1768 to replace the township of Killarow which was inconveniently close to the policies of the big house. The old township lacked many of the amenities of the new, which was supplied with running water, access to the sea and garden plots. It also had a new parish church, crowning the hill at the top of the main street. Built in 1767 in advance of the housing, it is highly distinctive, circular, so that the devil had no corners to hide in and with a tower and belfry built in dressed ashlar to contrast with the harling of the main body of the kirk.

The church can be seen atop its hill in the background of this picture of Bowmore Pier taken in 1946 just after the end of the Second World War. During the war, when flying boats were based on Loch Indaal, the pier was strengthened with concrete and topped with a concrete wall to protect it from the kind of wild weather that can afflict the loch and which made the military men reconsider its suitability as a base for their aircraft. The wartime concrete improvements overlaid the old rubble pier that was built in 1795 to replace a smaller original. Although quite long, the pier did not reach deep enough water for large vessels to come alongside and so these had to stand off while a craft known as the Bowmore Ferry shuttled between shore and ship carrying goods. In recent years the little harbour created by the pier has been equipped with pontoons for leisure craft of usually more modest dimensions than the launch seen here being serviced, and admired by little boys.

Bridgend is a delightful spot, picturesque, verdant and more akin to softer parts of the mainland than the Hebrides. It is seen here in a view looking across the hotel to the main part of the village, with Islay House nestling amongst the trees in the distance. Situated beside the Bowmore road, the hotel was originally an inn dating from the mid-19th century. The gardens in this picture appear to be planted with fruit and vegetables, to provide guests with fresh produce. Sadly, hotel guests have been unable to sample a whisky made at Bridgend, although a couple of attempts at distilling were made, once in the mid-18th century and again around 1820, but neither made a lasting impact. Somewhat heretically in the early 19th century there was a brewery at Bridgend producing beers that some observers hoped would encourage whisky drinkers to swap beverages.

Bridgend is Islay's geographical centre, a hub with roads, like the one being carried over the River Sorn on the bridge in this picture, radiating to all parts. Initially people moved around on drove roads or tracks beaten by countless feet or the hooves of horses carrying packs or panniers. Improvements began during the 18th century under the auspices of the Campbell lairds, with people having to give three days of their time, as a condition of their tenancies, to make and mend the highways. The road between Bridgend and the Port Askaig ferries was first to be upgraded followed by the one down the Rinns of Islay. That was helped by a small grant from the Commissioners for Highland Roads and Bridges, which had been set up in 1803 to improve highland infrastructure. People travelling to and from Kildalton tended to use the beach until a new road was made. When that was duplicated during the famine years of the 1840s, the island's basic road structure had been established.

With all roads leading to Bridgend, it was the natural place for the Islay, Jura and Colonsay Agricultural Association to hold their annual show, one of the highlights of the island year. The show field is seen here in a picture from the Edwardian period. With roots in an earlier society, the association was formed in 1838 with the improvement of livestock breeds as a founding aim. The Islay Show was one way that they did this. When the association was formed, the Islay landscape was already different from other Hebridean islands and the process of change was continuing, prompted by the reforms implemented by the Campbell lairds. By creating towns and villages like Port Ellen and Bowmore, they provided an alternative to the grindingly hard life of subsistence farming. Their actions can be characterised as a form of clearance, or as agricultural improvement, but either way it seemed to work on Islay.

Prior to moving into the towns, people lived in townships. These consisted of little more than groups of houses surrounded by ground where crops or vegetables were grown, with rough grazing land beyond. It was typical of the way Highland society was structured, but it was a precarious existence often made worse by sub-letting and it trapped people on the edge of starvation. As the impoverished rural population moved into the towns, larger farms were created. These became much more a feature of the Islay landscape than elsewhere in the highlands, a fact emphasised by the marginal impact of crofting on the island. As well as being something of a social event the Islay Show has, over the years, showcased agricultural excellence as seen in this picture, used as a postcard in 1931. Its title, 'Highlanders at the Islay Show', could refer either to the fine fat cattle or the kilted gentleman scrutinising them.

Having ousted the Macdonalds, the Campbells of Cawder (or Calder depending on which spelling is preferred) did little to establish a presence on the island until 1677 when Sir Hugh Campbell set about building the first bit of what became Islay House. He died in 1716 and ten years later Daniel Campbell of Shawfield bought the island estate. Originally from Kintyre, he was also heavily involved in Glasgow's mercantile life and brought this combination of influences to bear on the island. His grandson Daniel continued the trend when he inherited the estate in 1753 and although he died young, his brother Walter kept up the tradition until his death in 1816. Walter Frederick Campbell, his grandson, followed and continued the reforming work of his predecessors until forced out by bankruptcy in 1848. During their time, the Shawfield Campbells developed Islay House into a grand mansion with stunning views of Loch Indaal, and with extensive gardens and steadings. It is seen here in 1904.

Walter Campbell, who inherited the estate in 1777, built on his grandfather's activities by developing the fishing village of Portnahaven at the southern tip of the Rinns of Islay in 1788. It was in an ideal location with a well-protected harbour and access to fishing grounds in all directions, but on a rugged coast, exposed to the open Atlantic, these were also dangerous waters. To make them safer the 95 foot high Rinns of Islay Lighthouse was erected in 1825 on the Island of Orsay, just outside Portnahaven Harbour. Designed by Robert Stevenson, of the famous lighthouse building family, it is seen here in a picture from the 1940s. Another famous engineer was involved in the design of the village church. Built in 1828, it was one of a number of so-called Parliamentary Churches, erected using government funds allocated to extend the reach of the Established Church of Scotland in the Highlands. The Commissioners of Highland Roads and Bridges, who were given the job, delegated it to their chief engineer, Thomas Telford, who modified the designs of his surveyors to produce standard cost-effective buildings.

Walter Frederick Campbell established a new village on the western shore of Loch Indaal in 1828 and named it Port Charlotte after his mother, Lady Charlotte Campbell, daughter of the 5th Duke of Argyll. It was intended to be a local centre and also be sustained by two main activities, fishing and distilling. These industries were modestly successful and kept going for the best part of a hundred years, but when both ceased around the same time the village was left with little to sustain it. Once described as a 'showy village' it was able to capitalise on being an attractive place in a wonderful location and cater for the tourist trade. One of the main attractions, for both the village and the island, is the splendid Museum of Islay Life located in the old Free Church building on the northern end of the village. Opened in 1977 it has a wealth of stories to tell and artefacts to support them. This picture of the village, with the distillery on the right, was taken from a spot close to the old church.

At one time Port Charlotte could boast two distilleries, one at nearby Octomore, which ceased operations about 1840, and Lochindaal Distillery, seen in this picture. Writing in the mid-1880s Alfred Barnard described the distillery as 'old fashioned', but 'compact and well arranged'. The granaries and malt barns were 'spacious', peat was the only fuel used for drying the malt and the kiln was floored with a 'very expensive' German wire cloth. To ship the barrels of whisky they were either taken to the nearby Bruichladdich Pier or lashed together with iron pins and chains known as 'dogs' and floated out to ships anchored in the loch. Closed in 1929, the distillery buildings have since been used as the location of the Islay Creamery, a youth hostel and natural history centre, while some have also reverted to their original purpose as bonded warehousing. A new Port Charlotte Distillery has been mooted, so hope, like a distillery's water supply, springs eternal.

Bruichladdich Pier, which was used for shipping some of the whisky from Lochindaal Distillery, was the principal pier for the Rinns of Islay. Cargo vessels operated by David MacBrayne provided a regular service between Glasgow and Islay, calling here. In the 1920s or early 30s, when this picture is thought to have been taken, the route was being worked by either the *Lochiel* or the *Clydesdale*, two boats of very similar appearance, although the one in the picture is thought to be *Lochiel*. The pier was also frequented by those little west coast workhorses the puffers, bringing in supplies for the local communities and also for the distilleries. Coal was one of their main cargoes. Fuel in the form of oil being delivered to the nearby storage tanks has continued to be handled at the pier.

The little puffers that delivered coal to the pier could have started their voyage in the basins of the Forth & Clyde Canal at Port Dundas in Glasgow, a place noted for its distilleries. One of these, Dundashill, was owned by John Harvey whose son William opened a new distillery in 1881 at Bruichladdich. This was not an ancient haunt of smugglers or a laird's improvement project, but was an entrepreneurial development complete with a new village. The distillery buildings were also all new and arranged in a logical grouping with the still house made to hold a design of stills favoured by William Harvey. Following his death in 1936, a succession of owners kept the whisky flowing until the 1990s when devotees looked on with alarm as the distillery lurched toward closure, but in the year 2000 new owners took it on and gave it another lease of life. Twelve years later, the business was bought by Remy Cognac and the future of Bruichladdich (or Brookladdie if the local pronunciation is deployed) looks to have been secured.

Kilchoman Parish Church is about half a mile inland from Machir Bay on the island's western shore. It was built in the 1820s on a site that goes back to early Christian times, but the building ceased to be used for worship in 1977 and has since become a roofless shell. Surrounding the church is a burial ground, where standing tall amongst the other stones is the handsome Kilchoman Cross which dates from the 14th or 15th centuries. Some other stones from the area have been removed to museums for safekeeping. A further half a mile inland from the church is Rockside Farm where the new Kilchoman Distillery filled its first cask in December 2005. For an Islay distillery to be located some distance from the sea, on a working farm supplying its own barley was as if an old craft skill had been rediscovered, so this new kid on the block is both distinctive and highly unusual.

Walter Campbell, laird of Islay between 1777 and 1816, sold parts of his land holdings, including Foreland, to his son, also Walter Campbell in 1814. About six years later Foreland House had been built. It was a modest mansion with buildings grouped around two sides of an open courtyard and is seen here in the 1900s. Industry came to Foreland in 1842 when a tile works was set up to the north of the house. It made drainage tiles, a vital element in land reclamation and improvement schemes. The Foreland works must have been one of the most important aspects of Islay's agricultural development. Although it was the only works of its kind in Argyll, it was set up at a time when tax and legislative changes had been put in place to encourage landowners to raise capital for land improvement. With its job done, the works closed in 1899.

On an island where most of the major population centres were created and given new names, Ballygrant, seen here in a picture from 1930, stands out as an old settlement site with a Gaelic name: Baile a Ghrana – town of the grain. The agricultural associations are clear, but Ballygrant was also the centre of a lead mining industry that was in existence in 1772 when an early traveller, Thomas Pennant, visited Islay and was impressed by what he saw. Although never on the scale of mines on the mainland, the industry thrived well into the 19th century. Evidence of Ballygrant's anteriority is not just confined to its name; the village is ringed by sites of archaeological interest like the hill forts Dun Cheapasaidh Mor and Dun Guaidhre, while Dun Bhoraraic, Islay's only known broch, is about a mile and a half to the east. To the north-west, is the ancient stronghold of Finlaggan.

Viking and Gael vied for supremacy in the Western Isles until Somerled, reputed to be the son of a Celtic father and Nordic mother, turned the tide against the Norsemen. Somerled's grandson was Donald, the first of the powerful Clan Donald that assumed the title, Lords of the Isles, during most of the 14th and 15th centuries. Travelling in their galleys, or birlinns, because the sea was a more certain highway than any on land, they ruled over the Hebridean Islands and much of the western mainland of Scotland as if it was an independent kingdom. The centre of this fiefdom was Finlaggan, where the lord's great hall stood on an island in a small loch. It was a place of decision making where councils met, but it was also the centre of feasting and perhaps much drinking of whisky. The lordship collapsed in civil war and when King James IV stripped the clan of its title in 1493 he effectively cut the men of this warrior society adrift. They found a new role, as mercenaries – buannachan – hired soldiers, selling their fighting skills to the highest bidder. One such warrior, thought to be a man named Donald MacGillespie, is seen on this carved grave slab buckling on his sword belt ready to do battle. The slab was removed from its grave in the chapel at Finlaggan, probably by treasure hunters some time in the 19th century, and then discarded amongst the ruins. Shorn of its once vibrant past, Finlaggan had become a quiet, out of the way place, until the Finlaggan Trust was formed in 1984 to bring the story to life and help to preserve the site.

The birlinn in detail from the foot of the grave slab.

Port Askaig was the island's traditional point of arrival and departure. Drovers taking animals to market had them ferried from here across the Sound of Islay to Jura. They would then walk through that island to Lagg where another ferry took them across to Knapdale on the mainland. David MacBrayne's steamers never used this so-called 'overland' route, preferring to serve Islay directly from Glasgow or West Loch Tarbert. In 1968, a new company, Western Ferries challenged the MacBrayne dominance when they introduced drive-on drive-off ferries between Kennacraig and Port Askaig. The service only lasted for a dozen years, but it introduced the concept of purpose-built vehicular ferries. This transformed transport not just to and from Islay, but on the island itself. Port Askaig is seen here from one of the traditional steamers with MacBrayne's mail buses lined up on the pier. In the foreground, behind the man with a rope, is a bollard made out of an old cannon, while in the background is the Port Askaig Hotel, which has moved upmarket since its days as a drovers' inn.

The steamer sitting alongside Port Askaig Pier in this picture is the *Islay*, the third boat of that name to serve the island. The first *Islay* was built in 1849 and wrecked in 1866. She was replaced the following year by a handsome ship with a graceful clipper bow, also named *Islay*. The owners of these boats remained independent until 1876 when they sold out to David Hutcheson & Co., the predecessors of David MacBrayne. *Islay* (II) remained in their fleet until she too was wrecked in December 1890. Her replacement was the *Princess Louise*, a large sea-going paddle steamer that had been working the route between Stranraer and Larne since being built in 1872. Bought by David MacBrayne, she was renamed *Islay* and worked the route between Glasgow and Islay, until she too was wrecked on Eilean nan Caorach (Sheep Island) off Port Ellen in 1902. Her short time in the MacBrayne fleet helps to date this picture to sometime between 1890/91 and 1902.

This picture looking across Port Askaig to Dunlossit House appears to have been taken at the same time as the one on the preceding page. The Dunlossit Estate was created in 1860 when a chunk of the former Islay Estate around Port Askaig was sold. It was sold again in 1868, but this time it included a new mansion, Dunlossit House, built in the Scots baronial style. New owners took over the estate in 1890 and the house was rebuilt in 1909 following a fire. There was another change of ownership in 1911 and two more before merchant banker Helmut Schroder bought the estate in 1937. His son Bruno inherited Dunlossit in 1969. The Schroder family have played an active role in Islay life, including donating large sums of money to the Islay lifeboat. The first boat, the *Frederick H. Pilley*, was placed at Port Askaig in 1934. Apart from a couple of years in the 1940s when the boat was at Port Ellen it has been based at Port Askaig. The fourth boat, the *Helmut Schroder of Dunlossit*, came on station in 1979 and was replaced in 1996 by a second boat of the same name.

Offering a complete contrast to Dunlossit's Victorian turrets and gables were these little cottages just round the corner from Port Askaig Pier. Roofed with thatch that appears to be growing nicely, the cottages were also quite different to the so-called 'black houses' of the northern Hebrides, where roofs usually sat on the wall head rather than overlap it. The houses also show distinct improvements from those described by Thomas Pennant in 1772. He wrote about 'people worn down by poverty' whose houses were 'scenes of misery, made of loose stones' and which had no chimneys or doors, only 'apertures permitting smoke to escape… to prevent suffocation'. He also described food being cooked over an open fire as being sufficient only for existence and not for a 'vigorous life'. Compared to all that, these cottages were indeed mansions.

All of the big Islay distilleries were situated on the coast. They had to be because, in the days before roll-on, roll-off ferries, the only way to get operational necessities in and whisky out was by sea. One of the most substantial distillery piers was at Caol Ila, situated about half a mile north of Port Askaig as the boat floats, but somewhat longer by road. The distillery was built in 1846, sold in 1854 and sold again in 1863 to the Glasgow firm, Bulloch Lade. They were responsible for building the pier and also, in the late 19th century the huge three-storied bonded warehouse seen on the left of this picture. The period before, during and after the First World War was a difficult one for distillers. In 1920, having struggled through this time, Bulloch Lade relinquished ownership. A few years later the Distillers Company took a controlling interest, but in common with other distilleries Caol Ila was closed during the Second World War, so that barley could be used for food.

Caol Ila, the name refers to the narrows of the Sound of Islay, wasn't just a newly-built distillery, it was a new village of workers' housing described in the 1880s by Alfred Barnard as 'comfortable dwellings'. He envied the healthy lifestyle of the people who lived and worked here. The village, with the distillery nestling below the cliffs, can be seen here in a picture from 1952. Back in production after the war, the pier was renewed in 1950 and then in 1972 the whole distillery was demolished and rebuilt with production restarting in 1974. It became part of Diageo when that company was formed in 1997. For much of its existence the product of Caol Ila Distillery was used for blending, but single malts have also been produced. It is difficult to know though if a 'blend' or single malt was being sold by the Dumfries-based merchant who printed this misspelled advertisement – coal instead of Caol – in the 1880s.

Bunnahabhainn Distillery and its associated village were built a few miles to the north of Caol Ila in 1881. Distilling began the following year and reached full capacity in 1883. Situated beside a beautiful bay, with spectacular views of Jura, this was an otherwise sparsely populated place with few neighbours other than the keepers of Rhuvaal Lighthouse another four miles further north. The road into it from other places was long and winding and as ever communication with the wider world was by sea. The pier was perhaps the finest at any of the island's distilleries. The original owners of the distillery were a Glasgow-based company, the Islay Distillery Company, which later amalgamated with William Grant to form Highland Distillers. Burn Stewart became the owners in 2003. The water was, according to Alfred Barnard, drawn from the outflow of Loch Staoisha and was 'such as delights the heart of a distiller, being of a soft peaty nature'. Modern descriptions have it without peaty influences being drawn from a clear, free flowing spring. Either way, Barnard's word for it can be applied just as well to the end product: 'delight'.

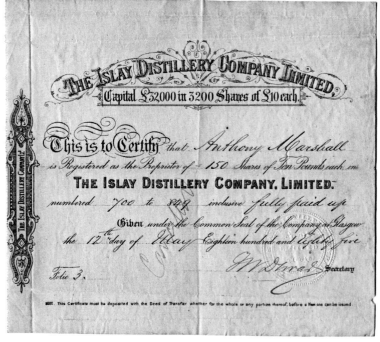